SHELLEY
THE CONCH

written and illustrated by
Katherine Orr

NATUREBOOKS

There are five kinds of conchs that live in the warm waters of the Caribbean Sea.

The *fighting conch* has a strong shell with a thick lip.

The *milk conch* has a lip that is often as white as milk.

The *hawkwing conch* has fine ribs on the back of its lip that make it look like a bird's wing.

The *roostertail conch* is so named because its lip is curved high like the tail of a rooster.

But the *queen conch* is the most beautiful of all. Its pink lip shines with shades of peach, rose and gold.

This book is about a queen conch.

hawkwing conch

fighting conch

2

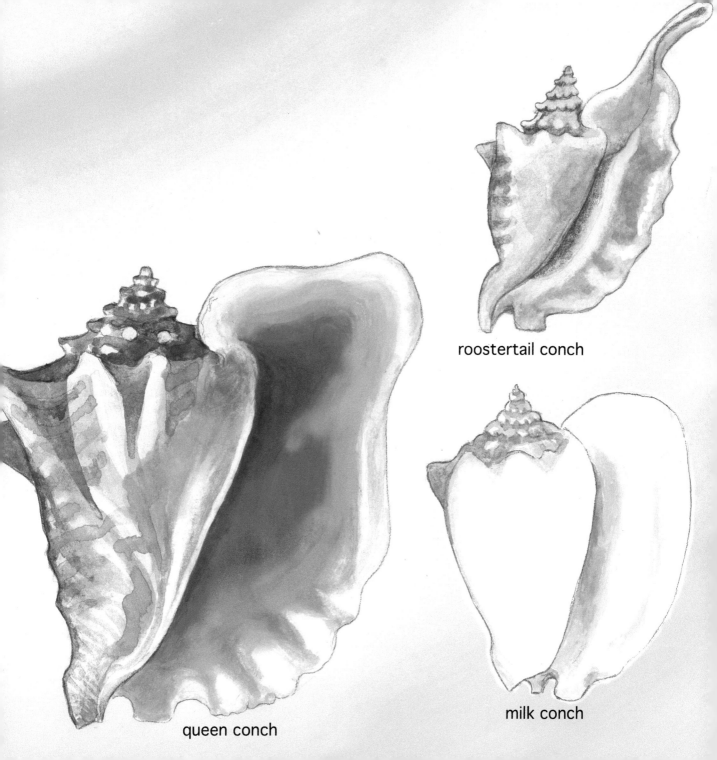

roostertail conch

milk conch

queen conch

Queen conchs are very special.
Their large shells are sold in stores all over
the world, and people wear jewelry made from
conch shells.
Their meat is sweet and white.
The people of the Caribbean have always
fished for conchs to help feed their families.
More and more people are fishing for conchs,
and conchs are now harder and harder
to find.
Who is the animal that makes this lovely shell
and feeds many people?
Let's turn the page and find out.

4

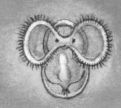

Shelley drifts in the warm ocean.
The waves rock her gently and the ocean
currents carry her.
She has just hatched from a tiny egg and her
clear body is only the size of a speck.
It is hard to believe that she will grow up to
be a queen conch, for right now she doesn't
look like a conch at all.
Her body has two round lobes like the ears
of an elephant. Each lobe is rimmed with fine
hairs that beat back and forth, very fast.
They move her up, down, and around in tiny
spirals and loops.

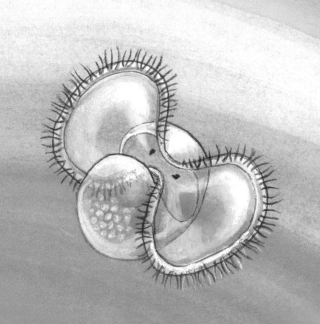

In the sea around Shelley are other tiny
living forms.
Some have soft jelly-like bodies and others
are glassy-hard.
Some are smooth and others have spines
and bristles.
Some will spend their whole lives adrift in
the warm sea.
Others, like Shelley, are babies.
They will drift in the sea only while they are
very young.
As they grow older their bodies will change
form and they will live their adult lives on the
sea bottom among grasses, rocks, sand, or
coral reefs.
These drifting animals and plants are called
plankton. Plankton means wanderer.
These animals and plants wander far and
wide, carried by the waves and currents
of the sea.

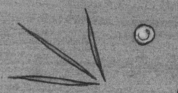

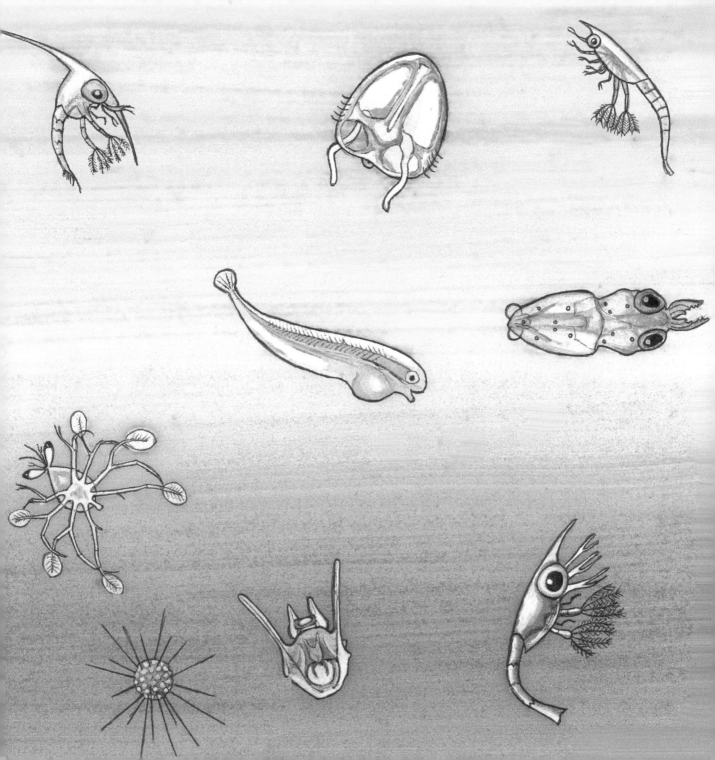

To Shelley's tiny black eyes, creatures the size of a rice grain appear as giant monsters who might eat her up.

These creatures in turn are eaten by larger animals.

The larger animals are eaten by larger ones still.

In this way, the plankton are an important source of food for many animals in the sea from fish to giant whales.

This is why vast numbers of babies hatch from eggs, but only a few of these many babies grow up.

Shelley will be very lucky if she can grow up to be a large pink-lipped conch.

10

Shelley spends her days drifting and eating.
The beating hairs of her two lobes bring
tasty bits of food to her mouth.
Shelley eats no animals.
She eats only plants.
She swallows each plant whole, so each plant
must be small and without hard coatings.
Her favorite plant foods are soft, bite-sized
globes of green.

Shelley drifts for about three weeks.
During this time, her two lobes become four
and then six.
Her body is now the size of a sand grain and
she is heavier, too.
She often touches the sea bottom before
bouncing up again.
Shelley finally settles on the sandy bottom
and then an amazing thing happens.
Over several hours her body changes form.
Her six lobes shrink and disappear.
Her mouth is now at the end of a long snout,
and her eyes are on stalks!
She is now ready to live on the sea bottom
as older conchs do.

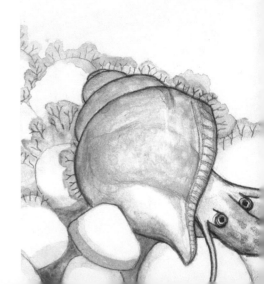

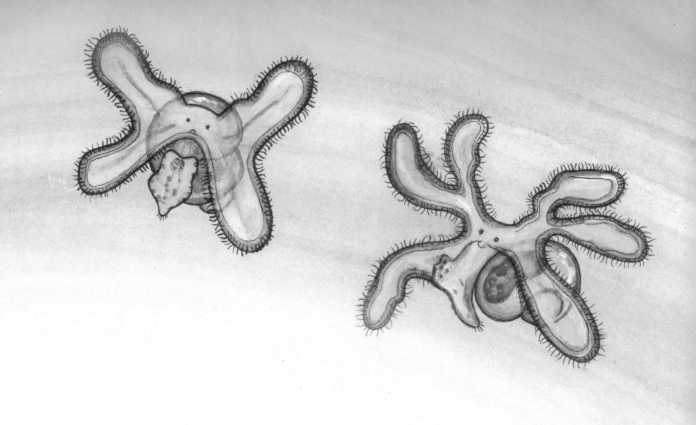

Beneath Shelley's white shell is a strong little foot with a flat 'claw' like a pointed toenail.

Shelley uses her foot to bury herself among the sand grains.

She is so small that she must hide from the many sea animals who would eat her if they could find her.

Here are some of the many animals that eat baby conchs...

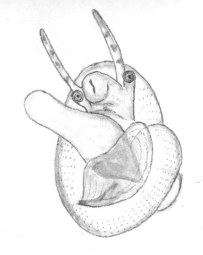

spiny lobs

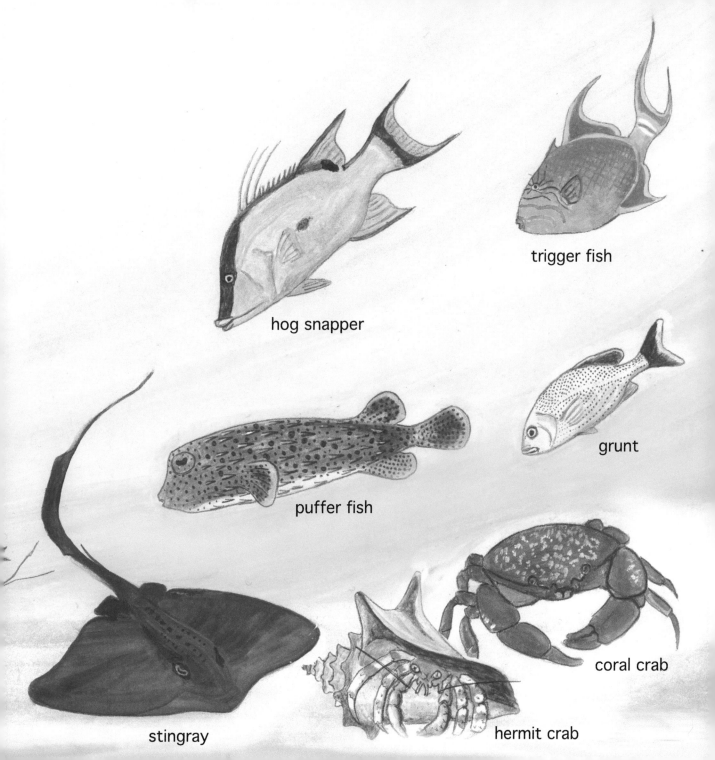

hog snapper

trigger fish

grunt

puffer fish

stingray

hermit crab

coral crab

Shelley hides for almost a year in the sand and under weeds.

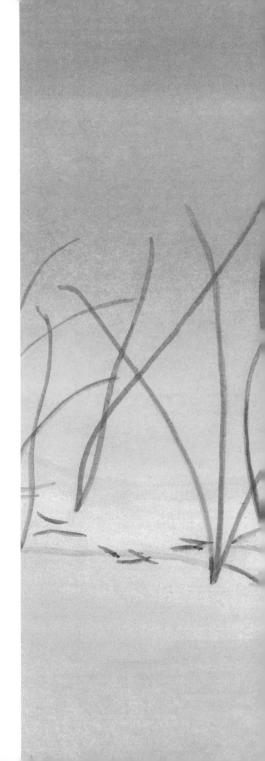

All the while Shelley is eating and growing. Her long snout can reach for food, and her special tongue is made for scraping.

With her 'tongue' Shelley scrapes into her mouth soft tips of seaweeds and fine films of dead plants and microbes that cover sand grains and grass blades.

Shelley will eat these soft foods for the rest of her life.

As Shelley grows she uses a special apron of orange skin to build a protective shell around herself.

Shelley's body grows in a spiral, so she builds her shell in a spiral too.

Her orange apron makes a liquid that hardens into new shell.

She adds strip after strip of new shell to the outer edge of her old shell.

This keeps a roof over her head and makes the tube wrap around itself as she grows.

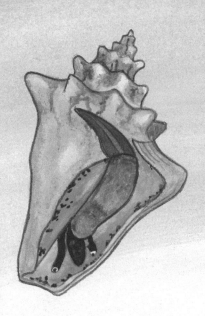

Biologists use special
names for Shelley's
snout: *proboscis*
tongue: *radula*
claw: *operculum*
and orange apron: *mantle.*

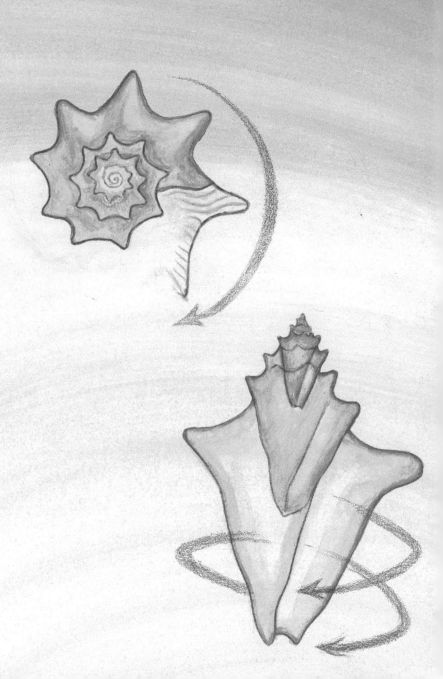

A year passes.
Now Shelley is big enough to move about in the open.
She sees other conchs around her.
Some are her size; others are much larger.
Some of the big conchs have lips that flare out like a spreading skirt.
One day, if Shelley is lucky, she will grow up and build a flared lip on her own shell.

Shelley is growing rapidly.
Her shell is now too thick to be crushed by a hog snapper or a puffer fish.
It is a safe home in which she can hide.
Her foot can also protect her.
When a tulip snail comes near her with the plan of eating her for its dinner Shelley kicks it in the face with her claw and leaps quickly away.
Both Shelley and the tulip are snails.
They are distant cousins.
But conchs, unlike most snails, have very good eyesight and can move quickly if they must.
Unlike other snails, conchs don't glide smoothly along the bottom.
Instead, they use their strong foot muscle to lift their shell up, thrust it forward, and take a step. Then they lift their shell up, thrust it forward, and step again.
To an onlooker, conchs appear to move about by hopping, or *leaping*.

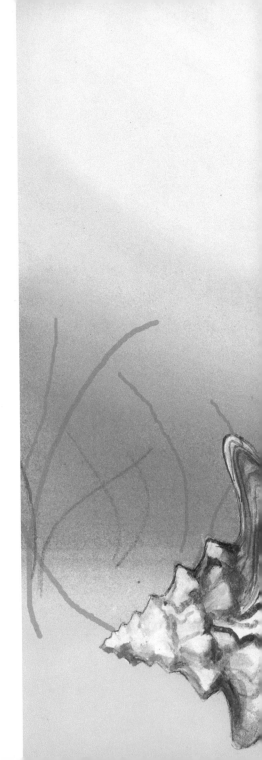

One day, a motorboat anchors near the spot where Shelley sits eating her breakfast of soft plant tips.

As her eyes look upward, Shelley sees a strange creature enter the water in a cloud of bubbles.

He dives down to the bottom and picks up two large conchs with flared lips.

He starts swimming towards her and Shelley withdraws her head into the darkness of her shell.

There is no way she can outrun this diver.

But nothing happens.
When she peers out again, the diver has passed her and is picking up another large conch.
He returns to the boat with his arms full of conchs and climbs out of the water.
Shelley does not know that she is safe from this conch fisherman because she is so small.
The fisherman knows that large conchs have plenty of tasty white meat in their foot.
He knows that he must let the little conchs grow bigger.
The fisherman also knows he must leave some adult conchs to breed and lay eggs so there will be more conchs in future years to feed his growing family.

The seasons come and go.
In summer the sea is warm and there is
plenty of food for Shelley and the other
conchs to eat.
Shelley wanders around the grass bed
eating, looking, resting, growing larger, and
building her shell spiral larger, too.

In winter the sea is cooler.
There isn't as much plant food to eat, and
Shelley and the other conchs don't move
around as much, or grow as fast.
Winter storms are common.
During these storms, Shelley buries her shell
into the sand and sits without moving,
sometimes for a few days, until it passes.
Sometimes adult conchs with flared lips dig
themselves into the sand and rest quietly for
many weeks.
Sometimes they lie still for so long that they
become covered with sand completely.

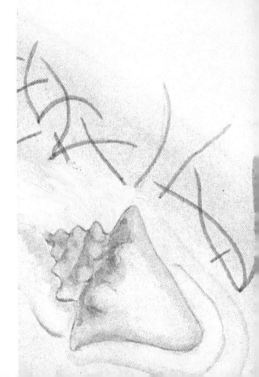

As spring arrives again, Shelley is almost
full grown.
She is two and a half years old and ready
to build a flared lip on her shell.
Without the need to make her spiral shell
larger, she now adds shell in a new
direction — away from her body.
Through spring and early summer she
adds more and more shell to her lip until it
flares like a skirt.
By mid-summer her lip is complete.
It is thin and fragile with a lovely pink
inside.

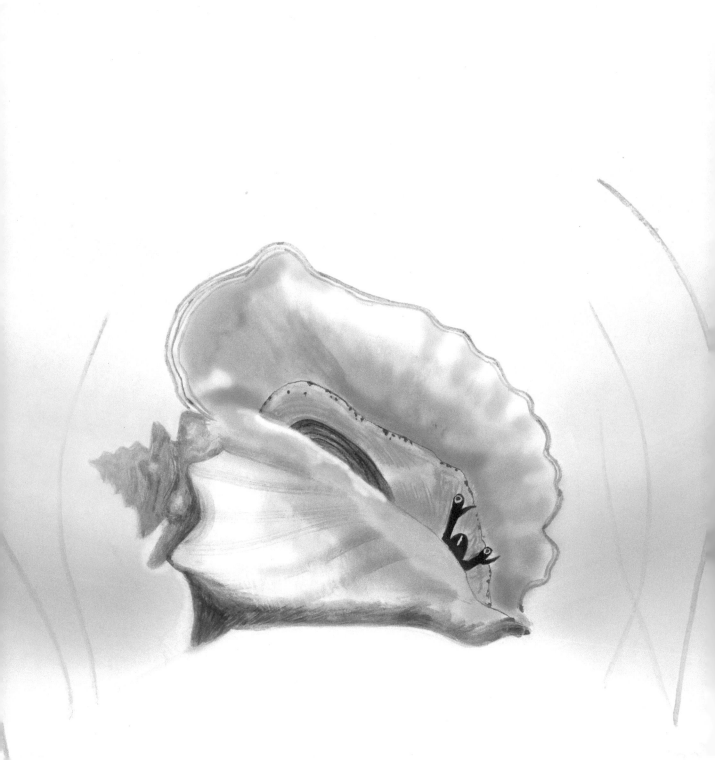

Now, after nearly three years, Shelley is as large as she will ever be.
Her shell will grow no larger.
Instead, it will grow thicker and thicker.
If Shelley lives to be very old (which for conchs can be anywhere from seven to twenty years or so, depending on where they live) her shell will have a very thick lip, and its outside will look old and worn.

Throughout autumn and winter Shelley makes
her lip stronger and thicker.
Now she is an adult, and one of the biggest
conchs in her group.
But she must still keep her amber eyes on
watch for enemies who might eat her.
Now her large kicking foot with its curved
claw can keep most crabs and tulip snails
away, but the loggerhead turtle can crush
her strong shell, and the octopus, stingray
and leopard ray can still eat large conchs.

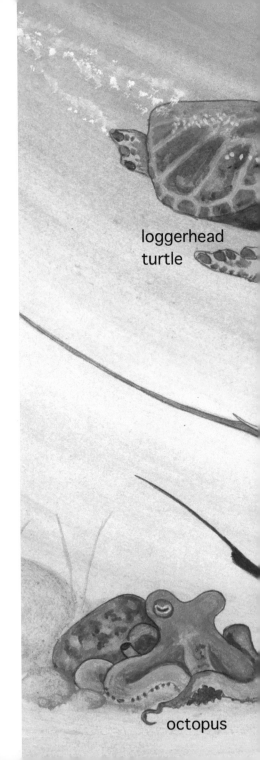

loggerhead
turtle

octopus

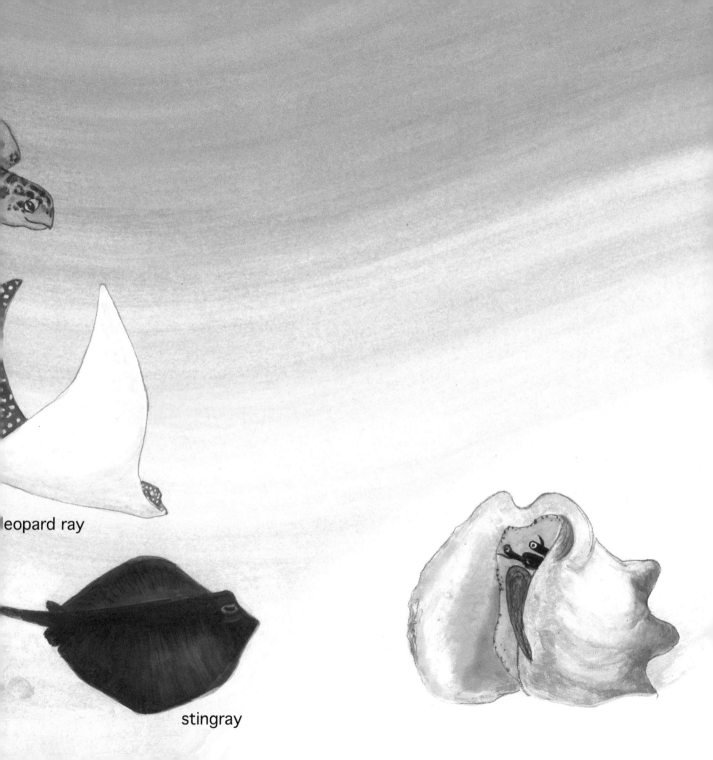

leopard ray

stingray

This spring when the sea starts to grow
warm Shelley moves away from the grass
bed where she grew up.
Now she moves with other adult conchs.
A male conch with a large shell and thick
flared lip moves close to Shelley.
They sit together with shells touching.
Under the shelter of their two flared lips
he reaches a special arm from his body to
hers and leaves her with many tiny seeds of
life.
Each one of his seeds will join with one of her
eggs to start a new life.
Later, Shelley will carefully lay a mass of
many, many tiny eggs.
Shelley will lay seven to nine egg masses
before the water turns colder again.

To lay her eggs, Shelley chooses a patch of clean sand where the sea is fresh.
There she sits quietly.
Down the side of her foot runs a special groove, and from this groove she lays a thin strand of clear jelly.
Inside this jelly are thousands of tiny white eggs, each the size of a pinpoint.
She moves her foot back and forth, back and forth, many times until the strand of eggs has formed a mass.
Grains of sand stick to the strand and when the egg mass is complete it can hardly be seen.
It looks just like a curved lump of sand.
Shelley leaves her egg mass to hatch by itself.
She does not need to protect her eggs or mother her babies.

egg groove

egg mass

The egg mass sits for three days on the quiet sea bottom.
The egg mass is still, but a tiny new life is swirling inside each egg.
In another day most of the eggs will hatch. New baby conchs will burst forth into the sea.
They will not look like big conchs yet but with luck a very few of them will live long enough to grow up and have strong shells with lovely pink flared lips.
As Shelley's eggs hatch, the circle of life becomes complete.

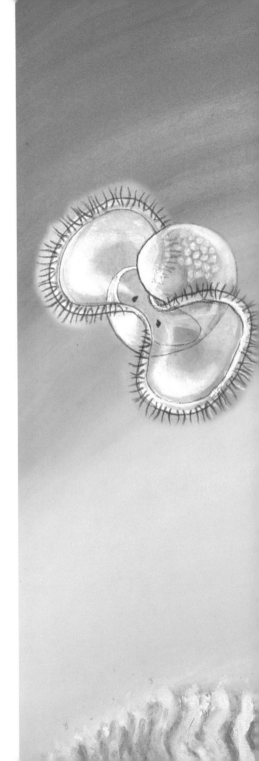

As long as the circle of life remains
unbroken it will continue on and on.
If we are very careful and keep the oceans
clean, and if we leave conchs untouched until
they have had time to grow up and lay eggs,
we will continue to have conchs to eat,
conchs to sell, and conchs to make more
conchs in the sea.

Originally published in 1984 by Macmilan, Ltd., London and Basingstoke
Multiple reprintings through 2010

First American edition published in 2015 by NATUREBOOKS, an imprint of
DragonGate Publishing, USA. www.dragongatepublishing.com
Published in the United States of America

Visit the author at: www.katherineshelleyorr.com

ISBN-978-0-9765178-6-3

Orr, Katherine Shelley
SHELLEY THE CONCH / written and illustrated by Katherine Orr

Summary: Readers learn about the life cycle and ecology of queen conchs through
text and pictures that trace the story of Shelley from her first days after hatching to the
hatching of her own eggs. Readers also learn the importance of protecting the circle of
life to ensure conchs continue on as a sustainable resource.

Printed in the USA

For more information on books by Katherine Orr visit www.katherineshelleyorr.com

CPSIA information can be obtained
at www.ICGtesting.com
Printed in the USA
LVHW071054291121
704732LV00011B/41